The Presidential Election

EVERYDAY LEARNING™

CHICAGO, ILLINOIS

Bibliography

Abramson, Paul R. *Change and Continuity in the 1992 Election*. Washington, D.C.: Congressional Quarterly Inc., 1994.

Barone, Michael, and Grant Ujifusa. *The American Almanac of Politics, 1996*. Washington, D.C.: National Journal, 1995.

Congressional Quarterly, August 19, 1995. Vol. 53, 33.

Corbin, Carol Lynn. *The Right to Vote: Issues in American History*. New York: Franklin Watts, 1985.

Fischer, Roger A. *Tippecanoe and Trinkets Too: The Material Culture of American Presidential Campaigns, 1828–1984*. Chicago: University of Illinois Press, 1988.

Hoopes, Roy. *Primaries and Conventions*. New York: Franklin Watts, 1978.

Melder, Keith. *Hail to the Candidate: Presidential Campaigns from Banners to Broadcasts*. Washington, D.C.: Smithsonian Institution Press, 1992.

Nelson, Michael, ed. *The Elections of 1992*. Washington, D.C.: Congressional Quarterly, Inc., 1993.

Schlesinger, Arthur M., Jr. *The History of American Presidential Elections, 1789–1968*. New York: Chelsea House Publishers, 1971.

Smith, Betsy Covington. *Women Win the Vote*. Englewood Cliffs, N. J.: Silver Burdett Press, Inc., 1989.

Data Sources

pp. 12–13, population figures: *The American Almanac of Politics, 1996*.

p. 13, dates of primaries and numbers of delegates: *Congressional Quarterly*, August 19, 1995. Vol. 53, 33.

p. 15, voter turnout 1828–1992: *Change and Continuity in the 1992 Election*.

p. 24, popular and electoral vote counts in 1888: *The History of American Presidential Elections, 1789-1968*.

pp. 24–25, electoral votes per state: *The American Almanac of Politics, 1996*.
The number of popular votes per state represent U.S. 1994 estimated voting-age populations from this source.

p. 28 voter statistics in 1992: *The Elections of 1992*.

Contents

Dear Student:

As you move through the Presidential Election *Storypath,* you may discover that you want or need more information about presidential elections. You can use this Sourcebook to find that information and to explore the election process further. This book is filled with photographs, drawings, charts, graphs, interesting facts, genuine news articles, and other documents from history that have to do with presidential elections. You can choose what topics you want to know more about and find them in this book. Read some or all of what you find on a page. Use the index inside the back cover to help you find specific topics, or let your curiosity guide you. Look at the diagrams on these pages to discover how to find information in this book.

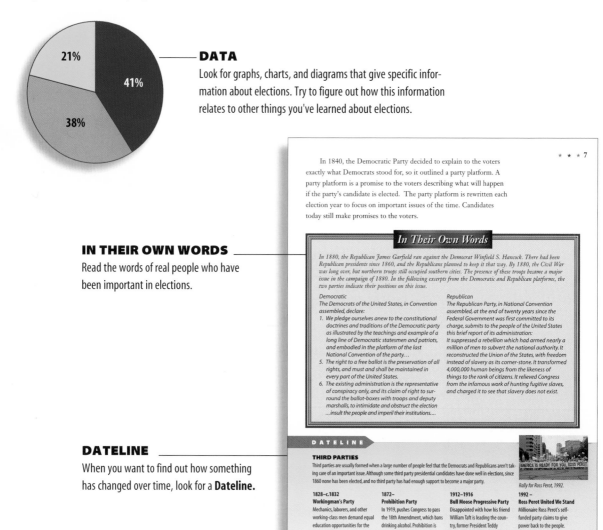

DATA

Look for graphs, charts, and diagrams that give specific information about elections. Try to figure out how this information relates to other things you've learned about elections.

IN THEIR OWN WORDS

Read the words of real people who have been important in elections.

DATELINE

When you want to find out how something has changed over time, look for a **Dateline.**

★ ★ ★ 7

In 1840, the Democratic Party decided to explain to the voters exactly what Democrats stood for, so it outlined a party platform. A party platform is a promise to the voters describing what will happen if the party's candidate is elected. The party platform is rewritten each election year to focus on important issues of the time. Candidates today still make promises to the voters.

In Their Own Words

In 1880, the Republican James Garfield ran against the Democrat Winfield S. Hancock. There had been Republican presidents since 1860, and the Republicans planned to keep it that way. By 1880, the Civil War was long over, but northern troops still occupied southern cities. The presence of these troops became a major issue in the campaign of 1880. In the following excerpts from the Democratic and Republican platforms, the two parties indicate their positions on this issue.

Democratic
The Democrats of the United States, in Convention assembled, declare:
1. We pledge ourselves anew to the constitutional doctrines and traditions of the Democratic party as illustrated by the teachings and example of a long line of Democratic statesmen and patriots, and embodied in the platform of the last National Convention of the party...
5. The right to a free ballot is the preservation of all rights, and must and shall be maintained in every part of the United States.
6. The existing administration is the representative of conspiracy only, and its claim of right to surround the ballot-boxes with troops and deputy marshalls, to intimidate and obstruct the election ...insult the people and imperil their institutions....

Republican
The Republican Party, in National Convention assembled, at the end of twenty years since the Federal Government was first committed to its charge, submits to the people of the United States this brief report of its administration:
It suppressed a rebellion which had armed nearly a million of men to subvert the national authority. It reconstructed the Union of the States, with freedom instead of slavery as its corner-stone. It transformed 4,000,000 human beings from the likeness of things to the rank of citizens. It relieved Congress from the infamous work of hunting fugitive slaves, and charged it to see that slavery does not exist.

DATELINE

THIRD PARTIES
Third parties are usually formed when a large number of people feel that the Democrats and Republicans aren't taking care of an important issue. Although some third party presidential candidates have done well in elections, since 1860 none has been elected, and no third party has had enough support to become a major party.

Rally for Ross Perot, 1992.

1828–c.1832
Workingman's Party
Mechanics, laborers, and other working-class men demand equal education opportunities for the poor and the rich.

1872–
Prohibition Party
In 1919, pushes Congress to pass the 18th Amendment, which bans drinking alcohol. Prohibition is repealed after 14 years. Prohibition Party continues to work to renew the ban.

1912–1916
Bull Moose Progressive Party
Disappointed with how his friend William Taft is leading the country, former President Teddy Roosevelt challenges him on ticket calling for reform in the White House and the nation.

1992 –
Ross Perot United We Stand
Millionaire Ross Perot's self-funded party claims to give power back to the people.

Sample page (page 9)

Today candidates can present their images and ideas on television and over the radio, reaching millions of voters. Airplanes make it possible for candidates to travel all over the country to talk to the voters. But before advances in technology made these techniques possible, many voters never saw the candidates in person or heard them speak. Newspapers and pamphlets displayed photographs of the candidates, along with their speeches. Because this was the only way voters saw the candidates, photographs were even more important in campaigns in the late 1800s than they are today. So, candidates posed for photographs that they thought would present the most popular image to the voters.

This button reminds voters of Teddy Roosevelt's experience as a Rough Rider, a special military group that fought for the people in Cuba. How would you describe Roosevelt's image?

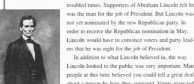

HISTORICAL RECORD

TO LOOK LIKE A PRESIDENT

In 1860, one of the greatest controversies in the United States was the issue of slavery. America was in search of a leader who could guide them through these troubled times. Supporters of Abraham Lincoln felt he was the man for the job of President. But Lincoln was not yet nominated by the new Republican party. In order to receive the Republican nomination in May, Lincoln would have to convince voters and party leaders that he was right for the job of President.

In addition to what Lincoln believed in, the way Lincoln looked to the public was very important. Many people at this time believed you could tell a great deal about a person by how they appeared. Voters expected candidates to look like strong leaders. Lincoln had two problems: he was not well-known to the public; and opponents of Lincoln used his appearance against him, claiming he did not look "presidential."

On February 27, 1860, Abraham Lincoln kept his appointment with the famous photographer Mathew Brady. Lincoln turned to Brady to make him appear stately, impressive, and presidential to the voting public. Brady wondered how he would make this tall, thin man look like the person who could lead the country through the blazing controversy of slavery.

Lincoln had big ears and a big Adam's apple. His neck was too long for his face and body. And on this February day, Lincoln wore a black, wrinkled suit that didn't fit him quite right. His tie was just a thin black ribbon, and his shoes obviously hurt him. Lincoln's shirt collar was loose and low, making his neck look longer than it was.

Mathew Brady would have to use all his skills as a portrait photographer to make Lincoln appear the strong leader of a nation in turmoil. Brady's first task was to rearrange Lincoln's shirt collar to make his neck look shorter. Brady had Lincoln stand for the photograph, with his left hand on a stack of books. Brady shot the photograph from the waist up so Lincoln would not look as tall.

In Brady's photograph, you cannot see that Lincoln's ears are large or that his suit does not fit. Lincoln looks like a man determined and noble in his cause.

Lincoln won the Republican nomination in May, 1860. This portrait of Lincoln was distributed on the first photographic campaign buttons, and Lincoln became well-known across the country. And on voting day, in November of that year, millions of people cast their ballot for the first Republican President of the United States, Abraham Lincoln.

Callout: HISTORICAL RECORD

HISTORICAL RECORD

Explore events from American history and learn about important people.

Sample section: The First Step: Primary Elections

The First Step: Primary Elections

Candidates try to prove to their parties that the voters like them. One way to do this is to enter state primary elections against other candidates from the same party. These primary elections show parties how voters in different states feel about the different candidates' images and platforms. Parties pay close attention to how many votes candidates receive in primary elections, especially in the larger states, to help them decide which candidate to nominate for President.

News Flash sample

January, 1988

News Flash

The Race Is On!

Next month, voters in Iowa and New Hampshire will pick candidates in special elections.

The election of the 41st President of the United States is not until November 8—ten months away. But politics is already a big part of the winter news scene.

Seven Democrats and six Republicans have declared that they want the job of President. In recent months, these major candidates have been hard at work running their campaigns.

Citizens Vote Their Favorites

February is an important month for the presidential hopefuls. That's when they begin to find out what people really think of their ability to lead the nation.

On February 8, both Democratic and Republican voters in Iowa will cast their votes on the first major statewide test of Presidential Campaign '88. On February 16, voters in New Hampshire will cast the second statewide votes of Presidential Campaign '88.

Over the next 18 weeks, other states will hold special elections. March 8 is called "Super Tuesday"

Democratic candidates, 1988.

because on that day millions of voters will show which of the candidates they

These special state presidential elections called *primaries* and *caucuses*. In these voters of the two major parties either p date or pick people who support a can way, the voters show which candidate

The presidential hopefuls will keep the primary and caucus voting. They w among them are the voters' favorites. some candidates who do not do well is New Hampshire will drop out of the p race.

From "The Race Is On" in WEEKLY READER ® 60 YEARS OF NEWS FOR KIDS, 1928-1988. Reprinted from Weekly Reader Corporation. Copyright © 1988 by Weekly Reader Corporation. All Rights Reserved.

Callout: NEWS FLASH

NEWS FLASH

When you want a new perspective on presidential elections from the past, look for **News Flash.** These genuine newspaper and magazine articles let you read about an event as if it has just happened.

Sample page (page 8)

What Does It Tak

Out of the many people who want to ru must choose only one candidate to repre paign. Many factors influence this tough qualifications for the office, which are w Second, the image the candidate present tant. Many things contribute to a candi platform, appearance, and social and pro Overall, the candidate's image must give or she can lead the country for the next

Campaign workers use many strategies to convince voters that their candidate is the best person for President. They choose characteristics of the candidate that they think will appeal the most to the voters. Then they present this image to the voters through photographs, slogans, and symbols on buttons, posters, and other items.

Did You Know? sidebar

Did You Know?

❓ 63% of our Presidents have been lawyers.

❓ 63% of our Presidents have had military experience.

❓ The average age of our Presidents upon entering office has been 55.

❓ The average height of our Presidents has been 5'9".

❓ John F. Kennedy was the first and only Roman Catholic to be elected President.

❓ Only two of our Presidents entered the office unmarried: Grover Cleveland and James Buchanan. Cleveland married while in office, and James Buchanan never married.

❓ 8 women have run for President as third party candidates. None has been elected.

Callout: DID YOU KNOW?

DID YOU KNOW?

Discover interesting facts about Presidents and elections in **Did You Know?**

Constitution excerpt

this delegate badge from the 1900 Democratic convention associates William J. Bryan, a Midwesterner, with farming. Why might this image help Bryan win votes?

United States Constitution
Article II

Section 1 ...No person except a natural born citizen, or a citizen of the United States at the time of the adoption of this Constitution, shall be eligible to the office of President; neither shall any person be eligible to that office who shall not attained the age of thirty-five years, and been

American Political Parties

Political parties are groups of people with similar interests and political ideas. Parties are organized to help elect candidates who represent those ideas and interests. In the United States, we have two major political parties: the Republicans and the Democrats. But it hasn't always been this way. When George Washington was chosen as President in 1789, he did not represent a political party or group. The founders of our country thought that political parties would cause arguments among Americans, as they did in England. But it was not long before Americans started to disagree anyway.

Democrat Woodrow Wilson and Republican Charles Evan Hughes try to win voters from the Bull Moose Party in this cartoon. (c.1916)

The first two political parties stemmed from a disagreement in Washington's cabinet. These parties, the Democratic-Republicans and the Federalists, did not hold organized campaigns. In 1828, Andrew Jackson became the first presidential candidate to organize his party. Jackson's Democratic-Republican supporters began calling themselves the Democratic Party. The Democrats created slogans and passed out paraphernalia to catch voters' attention. Being organized paid off, and Jackson won the election. His opponents then began to organize their party for the next election, and a two-party system was born in America.

The Democratic Party believes that it's the federal government's job to solve national problems like poverty and unemployment. The Democratic Party is often seen as the "party of the people" and has introduced many federal programs to help people, including Medicare and Social Security. The Democrats came from one of the first American political parties. Although the party has changed over time, its ideas about government have remained basically the same. Its symbol is the donkey.

The Republican Party believes that state governments and private organizations should solve problems like poverty. Many Republican programs favor big businesses. The party believes that as businesses make more money, they will create more jobs. The Republican Party was formed as a third party in 1854 by abolitionists who felt that the Democrats and the Whigs could not stop the spread of slavery. In 1860, the Republican Abraham Lincoln became President, and the Republican Party became the second major political party in America. Its symbol is the elephant.

These basic descriptions discuss general differences between party beliefs, not voters' beliefs. Typically, a voter's political ideas are much more complex.

In 1840, the Democratic Party decided to explain to the voters exactly what Democrats stood for, so it outlined a party platform. A party platform is a promise to the voters describing what will happen if the party's candidate is elected. The party platform is rewritten each election year to focus on important issues of the time. Candidates today still make promises to the voters.

In Their Own Words

In 1880, the Republican James Garfield ran against the Democrat Winfield S. Hancock. There had been Republican presidents since 1860, and the Republicans planned to keep it that way. By 1880, the Civil War was long over, but northern troops still occupied southern cities. The presence of these troops became a major issue in the campaign of 1880. In the following excerpts from the Democratic and Republican platforms, the two parties indicate their positions on this issue.

Democratic
The Democrats of the United States, in Convention assembled, declare:
1. We pledge ourselves anew to the constitutional doctrines and traditions of the Democratic party as illustrated by the teachings and example of a long line of Democratic statesmen and patriots, and embodied in the platform of the last National Convention of the party....
5. The right to a free ballot is the preservation of all rights, and must and shall be maintained in every part of the United States.
6. The existing administration is the representative of conspiracy only, and its claim of right to surround the ballot-boxes with troops and deputy marshalls, to intimidate and obstruct the election …insult the people and imperil their institutions....

Republican
The Republican Party, in National Convention assembled, at the end of twenty years since the Federal Government was first committed to its charge, submits to the people of the United States this brief report of its administration:
It suppressed a rebellion which had armed nearly a million of men to subvert the national authority. It reconstructed the Union of the States, with freedom instead of slavery as its corner-stone. It transformed 4,000,000 human beings from the likeness of things to the rank of citizens. It relieved Congress from the infamous work of hunting fugitive slaves, and charged it to see that slavery does not exist.

DATELINE

Rally for Ross Perot, 1992.

THIRD PARTIES

Third parties are usually formed when a large number of people feel that the Democrats and Republicans aren't taking care of an important issue. Although some third party presidential candidates have done well in elections, since 1860 none has been elected, and no third party has had enough support to become a major party.

1828–c.1832
Workingman's Party
Mechanics, laborers, and other working-class men demand equal education opportunities for the poor and the rich.

1872–
Prohibition Party
In 1919, pushes Congress to pass the 18th Amendment, which bans drinking alcohol. Prohibition is repealed after 14 years. Prohibition Party continues to work to renew the ban.

1912–1916
Bull Moose Progressive Party
Disappointed with how his friend William Taft is leading the country, former President Teddy Roosevelt challenges him on ticket calling for reform in the White House and the nation.

1992 –
Ross Perot United We Stand
Millionaire Ross Perot's self-funded party claims to give power back to the people.

What Does It Take to Be President?

Out of the many people who want to run for President, each party must choose only one candidate to represent it in the national campaign. Many factors influence this tough decision. First, there are legal qualifications for the office, which are written in the Constitution. Second, the image the candidate presents to the voters is also important. Many things contribute to a candidate's image, such as his or her platform, appearance, and social and professional backgrounds. Overall, the candidate's image must give the voters confidence that he or she can lead the country for the next four years.

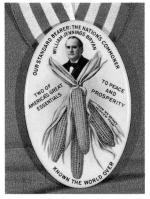

This delegate badge from the 1908 Democratic convention associates William J. Bryan, a Midwesterner, with farming. Why might this image help Bryan win votes?

Campaign workers use many strategies to convince voters that their candidate is the best person for President. They choose characteristics of the candidate that they think will appeal the most to the voters. Then they present this image to the voters through photographs, slogans, and symbols on buttons, posters, and other items.

Did You Know?

- ❓ 63% of our Presidents have been lawyers.

- ❓ 63% of our Presidents have had military experience.

- ❓ The average age of our Presidents upon entering office has been 55.

- ❓ The average height of our Presidents has been 5'9".

- ❓ John F. Kennedy was the first and only Roman Catholic to be elected President.

- ❓ Only two of our Presidents entered the office unmarried: Grover Cleveland and James Buchanan. Cleveland married while in office, and James Buchanan never married.

- ❓ 8 women have run for President as third party candidates. None has been elected.

United States Constitution
Article II

Section 1 ...No person except a natural born citizen, or a citizen of the United States at the time of the adoption of this Constitution, shall be eligible to the office of President; neither shall any person be eligible to that office who shall not attained the age of thirty-five years, and been fourteen years a resident within the United States.

Candidates must satisfy certain legal requirements before they can run for President.

Today candidates can present their images and ideas on television and over the radio, reaching millions of voters. Airplanes make it possible for candidates to travel all over the country to talk to the voters. But before advances in technology made these techniques possible, many voters never saw the candidates in person or heard them speak. Newspapers and pamphlets displayed photographs of the candidates, along with their speeches. Because this was the only way voters saw the candidates, photographs were even more important in campaigns in the late 1800s than they are today. So, candidates posed for photographs that they thought would present the most popular image to the voters.

This button reminds voters of Teddy Roosevelt's experience as a Rough Rider, a special military group that fought for the people in Cuba. How would you describe Roosevelt's image?

HISTORICAL RECORD

TO LOOK LIKE A PRESIDENT

In 1860, one of the greatest controversies in the United States was the issue of slavery. America was in search of a leader who could guide them through these troubled times. Supporters of Abraham Lincoln felt he was the man for the job of President. But Lincoln was not yet nominated by the new Republican party. In order to receive the Republican nomination in May, Lincoln would have to convince voters and party leaders that he was right for the job of President.

In addition to what Lincoln believed in, the way Lincoln looked to the public was very important. Many people at this time believed you could tell a great deal about a person by how they appeared. Voters expected candidates to look like strong leaders. Lincoln had two problems: he was not well-known to the public; and opponents of Lincoln used his appearance against him, claiming he did not look "presidential."

On February 27, 1860, Abraham Lincoln kept his appointment with the famous photographer Mathew Brady. Lincoln turned to Brady to make him appear stately, impressive, and presidential to the voting public. Brady wondered how he would make this tall, thin man look like the person who could lead the country through the blazing controversy of slavery.

Lincoln had big ears and a big Adam's apple. His neck was too long for his face and body. And on this February day, Lincoln wore a black, wrinkled suit that didn't fit him quite right. His tie was just a thin black ribbon, and his shoes obviously hurt him. Lincoln's shirt collar was loose and low, making his neck look longer than it was.

Mathew Brady would have to use all his skills as a portrait photographer to make Lincoln appear the strong leader of a nation in turmoil. Brady's first task was to rearrange Lincoln's shirt collar to make his neck look shorter. Brady had Lincoln stand for the photograph, with his left hand on a stack of books. Brady shot the photograph from the waist up so Lincoln would not look as tall.

In Brady's photograph, you cannot see that Lincoln's ears are large or that his suit does not fit. Lincoln looks like a man determined and noble in his cause.

Lincoln won the Republican nomination in May, 1860. This portrait of Lincoln was distributed on the first photographic campaign buttons, and Lincoln became well-known across the country. And on voting day, in November of that year, millions of people cast their ballot for the first Republican President of the United States, Abraham Lincoln.

In Their Own Words

In 1940, Franklin Delano Roosevelt ran for his third consecutive term as President. He was the first and last President in our history to serve more than two terms. FDR first came to office in 1933, during the Great Depression, and immediately set out to keep his campaign promise of "Change." The first few months of his presidency are known as "The Hundred Days." In this short time period, Roosevelt started his New Deal program to solve the economic problems that faced the nation. New Deal agencies created jobs for the unemployed, gave aid to struggling farmers, and strengthened the value of American money. In 1940, World War II was raging in Europe, and America's foreign policy became a central issue in this election. In addition, the New Deal programs were still new and needed continued support to grow. Following are excerpts from Roosevelt's last speech of the campaign of 1940, in which he tried to rally support for his foreign policy and continue support for his New Deal programs.

Cleveland, Ohio
November 2, 1940

Mr. Chairman, ladies and gentlemen:
    In making this, my final national address of the campaign, I express once more my deep regret that I could not carry out my wish to go to other States in the great Middle West, in the South and across the Mississippi River. It has been solely in the interest of peace and the maintenance of peace that your great Secretary of State and I have felt that we should both remain within easy distance of the National Capital in these trying days.
    Tonight in Cleveland, I am happy, through this great audience of my old friends, to give this message to America....
    The American people have faced with courage the most severe problems of all of our modern history.
    The start toward a solution of these problems had to be made seven years ago by providing the bare necessities of life—food and shelter and clothing. The American people insisted that those obligations were a concern of Government; they denied that the only solution was the poorhouse.
    Your Government assumed its proper function as the working representative of the average men and women of America. And the reforms in our social structure that we have achieved—these permanent reforms are your achievement.
    The New Deal has been the creation of you, the American people.
    You provided work for free men and women in America who could find no work.
    Idle men were given the opportunity on roads to be built, homes to be erected, rivers to be harnessed, power to be made for farm and home and industry....
    For the youth of the land you provided chances for jobs and for education. And for old age itself you provided security and rest....
    The task which this generation had to do has been begun. The forward march of democracy is under way. Its advance must not and will not stop.
    During those years while our democracy moved forward, your Government has worked with you and for you. Your Government has at times been checked. But always, with the aid and the counsel of all the people, we have resumed our march....
    And through it all there have been two thoughts uppermost in my mind—to preserve peace in our land; and to make the forces of democracy work for the benefit of the common people of America....
    We will make it—we will make it before the next term is over.
    We will make it; and the world, we hope, will make it, too.

The First Step: Primary Elections

Candidates try to prove to their parties that the voters like them. One way to do this is to enter state primary elections against other candidates from the same party. These primary elections show parties how voters in different states feel about the different candidates' images and platforms. Parties pay close attention to how many votes candidates receive in primary elections, especially in the larger states, to help them decide which candidate to nominate for President.

January, 1988 ## News Flash

The Race Is On!

Next month, voters in Iowa and New Hampshire will pick candidates in special elections.

The election of the 41st President of the United States is not until November 8—ten months away. But politics is already a big part of the winter news scene.

Seven Democrats and six Republicans have declared that they want the job of President. In recent months, these major candidates have been hard at work running their campaigns.

Citizens Vote Their Favorites

February is an important month for the presidential hopefuls. That's when they begin to find out what people really think of their ability to lead the nation.

On February 8, both Democratic and Republican voters in Iowa will cast their votes on the first major statewide test of Presidential Campaign '88. On February 16, voters in New Hampshire will cast the second statewide votes of Presidential Campaign '88.

Over the next 18 weeks, other states will hold special elections. March 8 is called "Super Tuesday"

Democratic candidates, 1988.

because on that day millions of voters in 21 states will show which of the candidates they prefer.

These special state presidential elections are called *primaries* and *caucuses*. In these elections, the voters of the two major parties either pick a candidate or pick people who support a candidate. Either way, the voters show which candidate they like.

The presidential hopefuls will keep a sharp eye on the primary and caucus voting. They will learn who among them are the voters' favorites. It is likely that some candidates who do not do well in Iowa and New Hampshire will drop out of the presidential race.

Primaries and Delegates

Most states hold primary elections between February and June of the election year. During this time, Democratic and Republican voters go to the polls to show which candidates they would like to represent their parties. In most states, only registered Democrats can vote in the Democratic primaries, and only registered Republicans can vote in the Republican primaries. When voters cast their ballots in these elections, they do not really vote for certain candidates. Instead they vote for representatives of the candidates, called *delegates.* The delegates with the most votes then go to the national convention in the summer and nominate the candidate they represent.

Candidates begin campaigning early in the year. They make appearances in the primary states, giving speeches and handing out paraphernalia in order to attract voters. The candidates do not have very much time, so they usually concentrate on the important states: the ones with the most delegates, and the ones with the earliest primaries. As the candidates travel from state to state, they have to pay close attention to the special needs of the different states and change their platforms and images to meet those special needs.

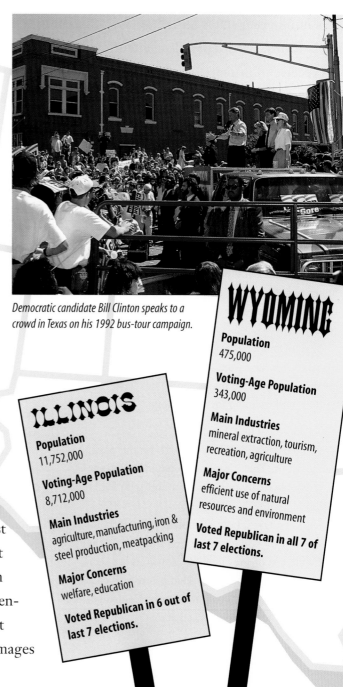

Democratic candidate Bill Clinton speaks to a crowd in Texas on his 1992 bus-tour campaign.

WYOMING

Population
475,000

Voting-Age Population
343,000

Main Industries
mineral extraction, tourism, recreation, agriculture

Major Concerns
efficient use of natural resources and environment

Voted Republican in all 7 of last 7 elections.

ILLINOIS

Population
11,752,000

Voting-Age Population
8,712,000

Main Industries
agriculture, manufacturing, iron & steel production, meatpacking

Major Concerns
welfare, education

Voted Republican in 6 out of last 7 elections.

NEW HAMPSHIRE

Population
1,137,000

Voting-Age Population
843,000

Main Industries
manufacturing

Major Concerns
economy, maintenance of low taxes

Voted Republican in 6 out of last 7 elections.

Texas

Population
18,378,000

Voting-Age Population
13,166,000

Main Industries
trade, service, manufacturing, construction, agriculture, petroleum

Major Concerns
crime, maintenance of low taxes

Voted Republican in 5 out of last 7 elections.

NEW YORK

Population
18,169,000

Voting-Age Population
13,646,000

Main Industries
manufacturing, finance, communications, tourism, transportation, services

Major Concerns
crime and taxes

Voted Democratic in 4 out of last 7 elections.

California

Population
31,431,000

Voting-Age Population
23,225,000

Main Industries
agriculture, manufacturing, construction, aerospace construction

Major Concerns
illegal immigration, affirmative action

Voted Republican in 6 out of last 7 elections.

Democratic and Republican Primary Dates & Number of Delegates for Each State, 1996		
	R	D
2/20 New Hampshire	16	26
2/24 Delaware	12	21
2/27 Arizona	39	52
North Dakota	18	22
South Dakota	18	23
3/2 South Carolina	37	52
3/3 Puerto Rico	14	58
3/5 Colorado	27	58
Connecticut	27	65
Georgia	42	91
Maine	15	32
Maryland	32	85
Massachusetts	37	114
Rhode Island	16	31
Vermont	12	22
3/7 New York	102	288
Super Tuesday		
3/12 Florida	**98**	**177**
Louisiana	**28**	**75**
Mississippi	**32**	**49**
Oklahoma	**38**	**53**
Oregon	**23**	**56**
Tennessee	**37**	**83**
Texas	**123**	**230**
3/19 Illinois	69	194
Michigan	57	158
Ohio	67	171
Wisconsin	36	93
3/26 California	163	423
Washington	36	91
4/2 Kansas	31	41
4/23 Pennsylvania	73	195
5/7 D.C.	14	38
Indiana	52	89
North Carolina	58	98
5/14 Nebraska	24	33
West Virginia	18	42
5/21 Arkansas	20	48
5/28 Idaho	23	24
Kentucky	26	61
6/4 Alabama	40	66
New Jersey	48	120
New Mexico	18	34
Montana	14	25

Voting in America

As different groups gained the right to vote, the number of eligible voters more than doubled. But voter turnout dropped. After fighting long and hard for this important right, many women, African Americans, and teenagers were not voting. Candidates realized that they needed to make some changes in order to get these groups to vote for them. They needed to address issues that were important to these groups. Advertisers and campaign workers also needed to make changes. They needed to design special items to attract the new voting groups.

Students are encouraged to register to vote at a special event in Tompkins Square Park, New York.

DATELINE

1789
In the Beginning,
there were many limits on who could vote. The founders of our nation thought that most of the population was not educated enough to choose good leaders. This meant that women, African Americans, and poor people couldn't vote. In fact, only white, male landowners who were over the age of twenty-one were allowed to choose the nation's leader. Soldiers from the Revolutionary War who were under twenty-one or did not own property wanted to vote, but they were ignored.

1848
July, Seneca Falls, New York
Lucretia Mott and Elizabeth Cady Stanton organize the first meeting for women's suffrage. Together with Susan B. Anthony and many others, these women realize that the struggle for equal rights begins with gaining the right to vote. At first, the women are not taken seriously. Many men felt that women had lower intelligence and should not be allowed to make such an important decision.

Susan B. Anthony and Elizabeth Cady Stanton, pioneers of the fight for women's suffrage.

1850
Property Requirements Eliminated
Almost every state allows all free, white males over the age of twenty-one to vote, whether or not they own any property.

1865
Slaves Are Freed
The 13th Amendment to the Constitution frees all African American slaves but does not give them the right to vote. This lets many white voters pass laws that keep African Americans from being truly free. People believed the freed slaves should have more education and own property before they could vote.

1869
Women in Territories Vote
Wyoming Territory grants women the vote, and other territories soon follow. Women in the territories worked hard alongside men to create a new life in the West. Men there believed that the women had earned the right to vote.

1870
African Americans Gain Vote
The 15th Amendment is ratified, giving African Americans the right to vote. Still, white racist groups use violence to keep African Americans from voting. Most states also require voters to take a difficult literacy test and pay a poll tax, which most African Americans can't afford.

In 1952, the Republican Party created paraphernalia designed to attract women to their candidate, Dwight D. Eisenhower. This dress sports his slogan, "I Like Ike." Can you think of other ways advertisers target women?

In 1901 Teddy Roosevelt became the first President to invite an African American, Booker T. Washington, to the White House.
In 1904, campaigners distributed this button celebrating the famous dinner in order to attract African American voters.

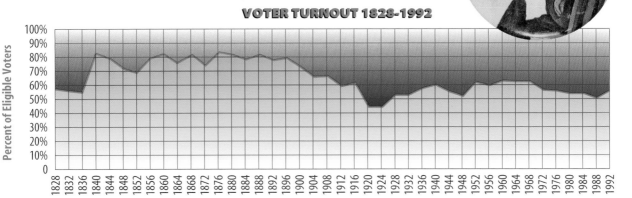

VOTER TURNOUT 1828-1992

(Graph: Percent of Eligible Voters vs. Election Year, 1828–1992)

What might have caused such high voter turnout between 1844 and 1892?
What might have caused the sudden drop in turnout in the 1920s?

African Americans vote at a southern polling station, 1867.

1909
NAACP Is Created
The National Association for the Advancement of Colored People works hard over the next sixty years for civil rights laws.

1910
First Women's Suffrage Parade
is held in New York. For the next ten years, women's groups give speeches, start women's newspapers, organize more marches, and picket the White House.

Suffragists march down Fifth Avenue in New York, 1911.

1917
Young Soldiers Want a Say
WWI soldiers under the age of twenty-one cry: "Old Enough to Fight, Old Enough to Vote."

1920
Women Win the Vote
Women's efforts are finally rewarded with the passage of the 19th Amendment, giving them the right to vote.

1965
The March in Alabama
Martin Luther King, Jr., leads a peaceful march from Selma, Alabama, to the state's capital, Montgomery. Police use violence against the marchers, attracting attention to the marchers' cause. President Lyndon Johnson pushes Congress to pass the Voting Rights Bill of 1965. Almost one hundred years after the 15th Amendment, African American citizens can finally exercise their right to vote freely.

1963
Young Soldiers in Vietnam
question the fact that they are not allowed to vote.

1971
Eighteen Year Olds Vote
The 26th Amendment is enacted, lowering the minimum voting age to eighteen. Unfortunately, many young people did not take advantage of the right. In fact, many young people still do not vote today.

Media and the Candidates

When candidates announce their intention to run for office, they are opening up their lives to public review. Candidates want the public to get to know who they are and what they stand for. But what information does the public really need to make informed decisions about candidates? Some people feel a candidate's personal life is a strong indication of what kind of President that candidate would make. Others believe candidates' personal lives have nothing to do with politics.

The media offer a great way to convey information about a candidate. Some people believe that scandalous stories about candidates are published to help one candidate look better than another. Others claim that controversial stories sell more newspapers, so the media are perhaps more eager to report negative stories about candidates.

As the 1996 presidential race began, the incumbent Democrat Bill Clinton was shown as indecisive and trying to cater to both sides.

August 21, 1984 𝔑𝔢𝔴𝔰 𝔉𝔩𝔞𝔰𝔥 ★ ★

Ferraro Denies Any Wrongdoing in Business

Rep. Geraldine Ferraro, the Democratic candidate for vice president, sought today to stem the criticism over her financial affairs, denying any wrongdoing but at the same time admitting that some mistakes had been made.

The tangled financial affairs of Mrs. Ferraro and her husband . . . have become a major issue in the presidential campaign. Earlier this week, she was quoted as being surprised to learn that her husband had borrowed $100,000 for their real estate company from the assets of an elderly woman whose finances he was overseeing.

In a two-hour press conference at Kennedy International Airport, Mrs. Ferraro acknowledged some sloppy record-keeping but insisted that neither she nor her husband had done anything wrong. She has released a huge mass of financial records.

"The supposition was that we had something to hide and obviously we don't," she said. . . .

Meanwhile, Walter F. Mondale, who just last month had handpicked Mrs. Ferraro as his running mate in the upcoming presidential election, voiced strong support for her today. "She's passed a test of leadership that will strengthen public respect for her and her capabilities," Mondale said.

Reproduced with kind permission of DK Publishing, Inc.

HISTORICAL RECORD

THOMAS NAST 1840–1902

Thomas Nast is known as the father of American political cartooning. In his cartoons, he commented on the affairs of his time. He used his cartoons to influence public opinion about candidates and politicians. Nast supported family values and fought against alcohol

abuse. His caricatures and biting comments led to many political reforms. His work also influenced the art of editorial cartooning. Many of his characters are still familiar to us today. He created Uncle Sam, the symbol of America. He also created the image we know as Santa Claus. Thomas Nast first used the elephant to represent the Republican Party and made the Democratic donkey symbol popular.

Voters must carefully decide which information they read about or hear on TV about candidates is factual, and which is opinion. News reporters are supposed to report only facts, but advertisements, for example, can use opinions to sway voters' choices. What are some other ways the media convey opinions?

Political cartoons are another way to influence voters' decisions. Political cartoons are created by private individuals who want to sway public opinion. In the 1800s, political cartoonists like Thomas Nast were very influential in the election process. Political cartoons are still a popular way to attract attention to an issue, but they are not as effective as they used to be. Why do you think political cartoons generally have less impact today?

In 1908, Teddy Roosevelt worked hard to help his friend William Howard Taft become President. But Roosevelt soon became disappointed with Taft and decided to run against him in the next election. Here Taft and Roosevelt are shown battling for the Republican nomination in 1912. How might this cartoon have influenced voters in this election?

The National Convention

In the summer of the election year, each party holds their national convention. The purpose of the convention is to vote on the party platform and to nominate the presidential and vice-presidential candidates. Each party chooses a convention city months in advance. The convention lasts for four days and brings excitement to its host city.

Supporters celebrate the nomination of Bill Clinton at the 1992 Democratic National Convention in New York City.

Conventions were first covered by radio in 1924 and by television in 1940. Before conventions were broadcast, they were only open to party members and delegates. Great arguments would often start over candidate nominations and platform planks. After each candidate nomination, supporters would celebrate wildly and bands would march down the aisles to show their support. It did not matter how rowdy the people were because the general public did not see what went on inside the Convention Hall.

When conventions became televised, parties realized that they would have to change their behavior to reflect a positive image before the television audience. They have also shortened the speeches, celebrations, and discussions so that the television audience won't get bored.

A delegate at the 1988 Republican convention in New Orleans shows support for candidate George Bush.

DEMOCRATIC AND REPUBLICAN NATIONAL CONVENTION SCHEDULE			
Day 1	Day 2	Day 3	Day 4
Introductory speeches	Make sure delegates were chosen fairly Vote on planks of party platform	Nominate presidential candidate Choose presidential candidate	Nominate vice-presidential candidate Choose vice-presidential candidate Acceptance speeches

★ ★ ★ **19**

In Their Own Words

George Bush
From the acceptance speech for the presidential nomination of the Republican Party at the Republican National Convention, Houston, Texas, on August 20, 1992.

I want to talk tonight about the sharp choices that I intend to offer Americans this fall: a choice between different agendas, different directions and, yes, a choice about the character of the man you want to lead this nation.

Four years ago, I spoke about missions—for my life and for our country. I spoke of one urgent mission—defending our security and promoting the American ideal abroad.

Just pause for a moment to reflect on what we've done....

This convention is the first at which an American President can say: The Cold War is over, and freedom finished first....

We offer a philosophy [for the next four years] that puts faith in the individual, not the bureaucracy. A philosophy that empowers [the American] people to do their best so America can be at its best. In a world that is safer and freer, this is how we will build an America that is stronger, safer and more secure.

The Vice-President

According to the Constitution, the Vice-President's only real duties are to be able to take over the presidency if anything happens to the President and to cast a vote if there is a tie in senate voting. Therefore, voters do not usually weigh vice-presidential candidates' qualifications as heavily as they do presidential candidates' qualifications. Still, presidential candidates need to be careful when choosing a running mate. Candidates usually look for a Vice-President who will help their image and appeal to a different group of voters. In addition, recent Presidents have given their Vice-Presidents more responsibilities than in the past. And many Vice-Presidents run for President themselves later.

VICE-PRESIDENTS WHO HAVE TAKEN OVER THE PRESIDENCY

President	Died in Office	Succeeded by	Re-elected?
W. H. Harrison	1841	John Tyler	NO
Zachary Taylor	1850	Millard Fillmore	NO
Abraham Lincoln	1865	Andrew Johnson	NO
James A. Garfield	1881	Chester A. Arthur	NO
William McKinley	1901	Theodore Roosevelt	YES
Warren G. Harding	1923	Calvin Coolidge	YES
Franklin D. Roosevelt	1945	Harry S. Truman	YES
John F. Kennedy	1963	Lyndon B. Johnson	YES
Richard M. Nixon	1974 (resigned)	Gerald R. Ford	NO

On the Campaign Trail

Shortly after the conventions, candidates begin their national campaigns. Presidential hopefuls have just two short months to achieve their goal. Parties use many techniques to introduce voters to their candidates. What are some of the ways you have learned about candidates?

Over the years, technology has changed the way candidates get their ideas out to the public. Nationwide television and radio broadcasts can reach millions of voters at once, while most newspapers can only target selected areas. Candidates can fly all over the country to give speeches instead of touring a limited area by train. Computers help campaigners work faster and more efficiently. Can you think of other ways technology has affected political campaigns?

Today, candidates do much of their advertising on television. Democrat Paul Simon used this commercial to attract support during the 1988 primaries. What might some disadvantages be of campaigning on television?

This unusual gadget was distributed in the election of 1896 to draw support for Republican William McKinley. Voters could spin this wheel to "discover" what would happen if McKinley were elected.

Campaign songs, which used words and music to emphasize the popular image of a candidate, first became popular in 1828. In 1920, supporters of Democratic candidate James Cox were encouraged to sing this song which emphasized his support for the League of Nations.

In the 1800s, a popular form of campaign paraphernalia was the ribbon, like this one from 1868, which supporters could wear on their jackets at rallies. Why do you think campaign ribbons are less popular today?

Warren Harding records a speech on the newly invented phonograph record to distribute his ideas to voters. (c. 1920)

DATELINE

1789
In the Beginning,
presidential candidates did not campaign. It was considered undignified to seek the office of President. Candidates waited quietly at home and were chosen based upon past statesmanship.

1828
Paraphernalia Is Used to Win Votes
Democrats emphasize candidate Andrew Jackson's military experience on a variety of buttons, banners, and gadgets designed to attract voters.

1840
The "Hurrah" Campaign
Voters participate in parades, rallies, and other events celebrating Whig candidate William H. Harrison. Whigs use more paraphernalia than ever before to entertain and influence voters. Harrison, hero of the battle of Tippecanoe, and his running mate, Tyler, adopt the first real campaign slogan, "Tippecanoe and Tyler, Too!" which appears on banners, buttons, and in songs. When a Democratic newspaperman says Harrison would be happy living in a log cabin with a barrel of hard cider, Whigs turn this attack to their favor by playing up the image of Harrison as a rugged, common man. Gadgets such as miniature barrels filled with cider are distributed to encourage more support.

Harrison and Tyler campaign badge.

1880
Railroads and Candidates
Candidates still do not actively campaign for themselves. But voters want to see their candidate, and railroads make this possible. Republican candidate James A. Garfield entertains daily visitors in the first "front-porch" campaign.

1904
Hitting the Campaign Trail
Republican Theodore Roosevelt breaks custom and takes his campaign out to the people. Roosevelt tours the country making speeches from the back of a train in one of the first "whistle-stop" campaigns.

1932
Radio Brings Candidates into the Home
Democratic President Franklin Roosevelt makes radio broadcasts explaining government policy to the people. Through these broadcasts, called "fireside chats," citizens become familiar with Roosevelt and his policies. This massive exposure helps Roosevelt get elected three more times.

1960
The Impact of Television
Candidates' images play a bigger role when millions of voters watch televised debates between Richard M. Nixon and John F. Kennedy. Newscasters begin interviewing candidates on TV. Soon, parties create commercials advertising their candidates and attacking opponents.

1996
"Surfing the Net"
Computers and the Internet open the door for new possibilities in campaigning. How do you think campaigns will change?

Presidential Debates

The First Great Debates

In the summer of 1858, incumbent Senator Stephen A. Douglas and challenger Abraham Lincoln engaged in a series of seven debates while campaigning for the office of senator of Illinois. The central issue was slavery, which was already dividing the nation and would soon lead to the Civil War. The debates were held outside, in seven different cities in Illinois. Huge crowds attended the events, cheering or booing after each statement. Supporters followed them from city to city. The two men spoke vividly and passionately, and their words were reprinted in newspapers for the rest of the country to read. Although Lincoln lost the senatorial race, he received more votes in the counties where the debates were held than he did in other counties. And the debates made Lincoln famous, so that two years later, he became the first Republican President of the United States.

How do you think the debates affected the candidates in these elections?
What differences do you see between the Lincoln-Douglas debates and the Kennedy-Nixon debates? What similarities?
How do you think technology affected the outcome of the debates?

Debating in Modern Times

In the campaign of 1960, Democrat John F. Kennedy battled Republican Richard M. Nixon in a series of four televised debates. Millions of voters watched the debates from their living rooms or listened to them on the radio. Voters watching the debates noticed that Kennedy looked calm and collected. He had just returned from campaigning in California and had a healthy tan. Nixon, on the other hand, was still recovering from a knee injury, leaving him pale and thin. In addition, he was sweating, which made him look nervous. Nixon wore a suit that made him look as if he blended into the background of the television studio's stage. Kennedy wore a darker color, so he stood out. People who watched the debates on television thought Kennedy had easily "won" the debates. People who listened to the radio had a different opinion. They had listened to the candidates' words without being affected by their images and thought Nixon had won.

The Electoral College

When voters go to the polling booth in November, they don't really vote for the President. Instead, a group of 538 men and women, called *electors*, cast the votes for this office. So why do people vote? The state's electors vote how the state's people want them to vote. The candidate who receives the majority of the people's votes (called *popular votes*) in a state gets *all* of the electoral votes of that state. This is known as the "winner takes all" rule. The President is then elected by the majority of electoral votes.

A candidate needs a majority of the electoral votes (at least 270) to win the election. But he does not need a majority of the popular votes. When a candidate receives more popular votes than his opponent but does not receive the majority of the votes, he has received a plurality of the votes. Twelve of our Presidents have been elected with a majority of the electoral vote but only a plurality of the popular vote. One President, Benjamin Harrison, was elected even though he lost the popular vote count. Do you think a race like this reflects whom the voters wanted for President? Can you think of a more fair way to elect the President?

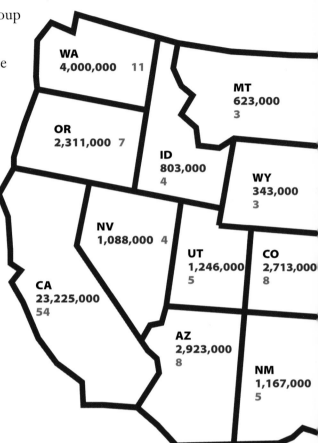

State	Population	Electoral Votes
WA	4,000,000	11
MT	623,000	3
OR	2,311,000	7
ID	803,000	4
WY	343,000	3
NV	1,088,000	4
UT	1,246,000	5
CO	2,713,000	8
CA	23,225,000	54
AZ	2,923,000	8
NM	1,167,000	5

HISTORICAL RECORD

It was the election of 1888. The Republican candidate, Benjamin Harrison, was the clear winner with 233 electoral votes. His opponent, the Democrat Grover Cleveland, only received 168 electoral votes. However, Cleveland received over 100,000 more popular votes than Harrison. How could the vote count be so different? Look at the chart below. In many states, the popular vote was very close. But, even when Harrison had only 1 or 2 percent more popular votes than Cleveland, he took all of the states' electoral votes.

Grover Cleveland

Popular v. Electoral Votes in 5 States
Election of 1888

	Popular Votes		Electoral Votes	
	Harrison	*Cleveland*	*Harrison*	*Cleveland*
California	124,816	117, 729	8	
Indiana	263,361	261,013	15	
Missouri	236,257	261,974		16
New York	648,759	635,757	36	
Virginia	150,438	151,977		12
5 state total	*1,423,631*	*1,428,449*	*59*	*28*

Benjamin Harrison

Each state is allotted a certain number of electors, equal to the number of its representatives and senators. Each state has two senators. The number of representatives for each state depends on that state's population. Each state gets at least three electoral votes.

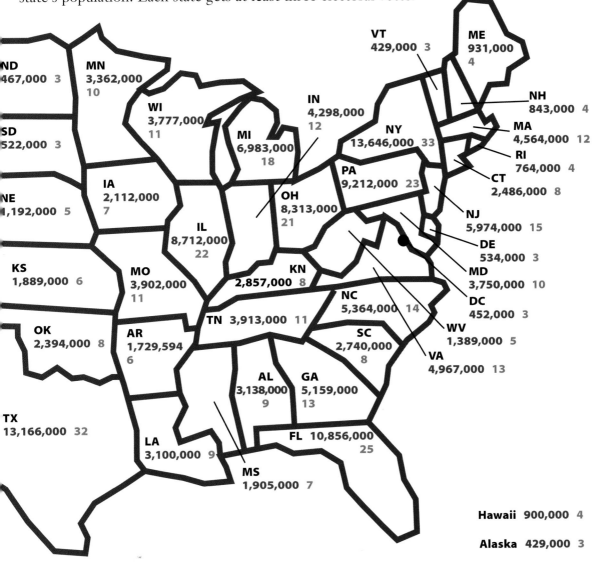

Hawaii 900,000 4

Alaska 429,000 3

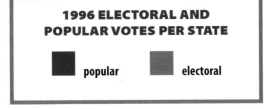

1996 ELECTORAL AND POPULAR VOTES PER STATE

popular   electoral

Inauguration and Celebration

The final step in the election process is the inauguration of the new President and Vice-President. This happens on January 20 of the year after the election. Every inauguration is different, depending on the personality and image of the new President. The inauguration is a celebration, but it is also an introduction of the new President to the country. So the type of inauguration held by the President is one very important way that the President can reinforce the image he or she projected throughout the campaign.

January 20, 1993: Bill and Hillary Clinton dance at one of twelve inaugural balls.

No matter what the tone of the inauguration, three events are always the same. First, the President and the Vice-President must take the oath of office, which is written in the Constitution. Second, the new President gives an inaugural address, a speech that reminds supporters why they elected him and what he promises to do over the next four years. Finally, the celebration ends with an inaugural ball.

January 20, 1961: The Kennedys greet guests at an inaugural ball held at the Mayflower hotel.

Jan. 21, 1989 𝕹𝖊𝖜𝖘 𝕱𝖑𝖆𝖘𝖍 ★

Presidential Style

A President's inauguration, they say, sets the style for his reign. Thus Jimmy Carter spent only $3.5m; walked back to the White House from his Capitol Hill swearing-in; and set the top price for tickets to the inaugural balls at $25. He was to be the people's president. Ronald Reagan wore a morning coat, spent $16m, and charged up to $1,000 for ball tickets. He was to be an elected monarch. . . . Thomas Jefferson held no party, walked to the Capitol in a plain coat and then retired to his boarding house. Eight years later James and Dolly Madison danced the night away in glamour and pomp.

From: "Fish Story" in THE ECONOMIST, January 21, 1989. © 1989 The Economist Newspaper Group, Inc. Reprinted with permission. Further reproduction prohibited.

George Washington takes the oath of office at the first American presidential inauguration. ▶

U.S. Constitution, Article II

Section 1. Before he enter on the execution of his office, he shall take the following oath or affirmation: "I do solemnly swear (or affirm) that I will faithfully execute the Office of President of the United States, and will to the best of my Ability, preserve, protect and defend the Constitution of the United States."

Voting Statistics from the 1992 Election

Statistics can be very important campaign tools. Look at the graphs below, which show how different social groups voted in 1992. Why might statistics like these be important? How might a candidate use these statistics to help him/her?

■ **Bill Clinton:**
Democrat

■ **George Bush:**
Republican

□ **Ross Perot:**
Independent
(third party)

BY AGE GROUP

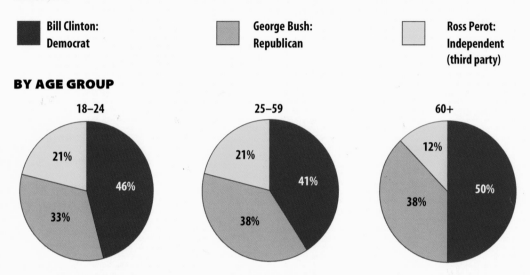

What similarities do you see in how the different age groups voted? What differences? What might some of the reasons be for these similarities and differences?

BY GENDER

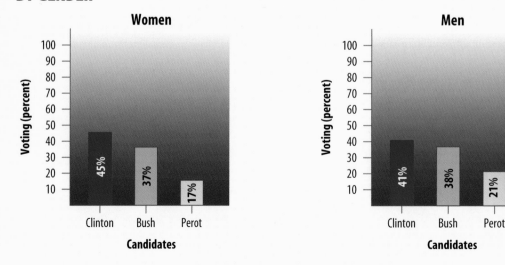

How did men and women vote differently in the 1992 election? Why might men and women vote differently?

The Three Branches of Government

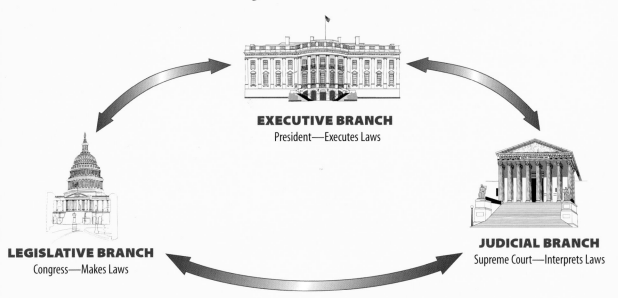

EXECUTIVE BRANCH
President—Executes Laws

LEGISLATIVE BRANCH
Congress—Makes Laws

JUDICIAL BRANCH
Supreme Court—Interprets Laws

GOVERNMENT BUILDINGS

* In 1792, George Washington offered $500 to whomever could create the best design for the Presidential House. Architects had three months to submit their ideas. Washington chose the designs of James Hoban, who went on to build the first version of what we call the White House.

* The Supreme Court building is nicknamed "the Marble Palace" because it is so big and beautiful.

* Members of Congress meet in the magnificent Capitol building, which sits on Capitol Hill. The great dome on top of the Capitol was constructed from almost nine million tons of cast iron! And the Statue of Freedom that stands on top of the dome is nearly twenty feet tall!

GOVERNMENT PEOPLE

* Supreme Court justices are not elected, they are chosen by the President. Unlike elected officials, these judges can serve as long as they want and are only replaced when they retire. One judge, Justice Oliver Wendell Holmes, Jr., held his position until he was ninety!

* Thurgood Marshall became the first African American on the Supreme Court. He was appointed in 1967. In 1981, Sandra Day O'Connor became the first woman to be appointed to the Supreme Court.

* Members of Congress (senators and representatives) get many privileges. When they need to go from their offices to Capitol Hill, they can ride a special subway that was created just for them. And when they want to send letters or advertisements to voters, they don't need to pay for stamps. Instead they just put a copy of their signature where the stamp should be!

Chronological List of Presidents in American History

President	Years in office	Party	Born-died	Vice-President
George Washington	1789–1797	none	1732–1799	John Adams
John Adams	1797–1801	Federalist	1735–1826	Thomas Jefferson
Thomas Jefferson	1801–1809	Democratic-Republican	1743–1826	Aaron Burr, George Clinton
James Madison	1809–1817	Democratic-Republican	1751–1836	George Clinton, Elbridge Gerry
James Monroe	1817–1825	Democratic-Republican	1758–1831	Daniel D. Tompkins
John Quincy Adams	1825–1829	Democratic-Republican	1767–1848	John C. Calhoun
Andrew Jackson	1829–1837	Democratic	1767–1845	John C. Calhoun, Martin Van Buren
Martin Van Buren	1837–1841	Democratic	1782–1862	Richard M. Johnson
William Henry Harrison	1841	Whig	1773–1841	John Tyler
John Tyler	1841–1845	Whig	1790–1862	none
James K. Polk	1845–1849	Democratic	1795–1849	George M. Dallas
Zachary Taylor	1849–1850	Whig	1784–1850	Millard Fillmore
Millard Fillmore	1850–1853	Whig	1800–1874	none
Franklin Pierce	1853–1857	Democratic	1804–1869	William R. King
James Buchanan	1857–1861	Democratic	1791–1868	John C. Breckinridge
Abraham Lincoln	1861–1865	Republican, Union	1809–1865	Hannibal Hamlin, Andrew Johnson
Andrew Johnson	1865–1869	Union	1808–1875	none
Ulysses S. Grant	1869–1877	Republican	1822–1885	Schuyler Colfax, Henry Wilson
Rutherford B. Hayes	1877–1881	Republican	1822–1893	William A. Wheeler
James A. Garfield	1881	Republican	1831–1881	Chester A. Arthur
Chester A. Arthur	1881–1885	Republican	1829–1886	none
Grover Cleveland	1885–1889	Democratic	1837–1908	Thomas A. Hendricks
Benjamin Harrison	1889–1893	Republican	1833–1901	Levi P. Morton
Grover Cleveland	1893–1897	Democratic	1837–1908	Adlai E. Stevenson
William McKinley	1897–1901	Republican	1843–1901	Garret A. Hobart, Theodore Roosevelt
Theodore Roosevelt	1901–1909	Republican	1858–1919	none, Charles W. Fairbanks
William Howard Taft	1909–1913	Republican	1857–1930	James S. Sherman
Woodrow Wilson	1913–1921	Democratic	1856–1924	Thomas R. Marshall
Warren G. Harding	1921–1923	Republican	1865–1923	Calvin Coolidge
Calvin Coolidge	1923–1929	Republican	1872–1933	none, Charles G. Dawes
Herbert C. Hoover	1929–1933	Republican	1874–1964	Charles Curtis
Franklin D. Roosevelt	1933–1945	Democratic	1882–1945	John Nance Garner, Henry A. Wallace, Harry S. Truman
Harry S. Truman	1945–1953	Democratic	1884–1972	none, Alben W. Barkley
Dwight D. Eisenhower	1953–1961	Republican	1890–1969	Richard M. Nixon
John F. Kennedy	1961–1963	Democratic	1917–1963	Lyndon B. Johnson
Lyndon B. Johnson	1963–1969	Democratic	1908–1973	none, Hubert H. Humphrey
Richard M. Nixon	1969–1974	Republican	1913–1994	Spiro T. Agnew, Gerald R. Ford
Gerald R. Ford	1974–1977	Republican	1913–	Nelson A. Rockefeller
Jimmy Carter	1977–1981	Democratic	1924–	Walter F. Mondale
Ronald W. Reagan	1981–1989	Republican	1911–	George H. W. Bush
George H. W. Bush	1989–1993	Republican	1924–	J. Danforth Quayle
William J. Clinton	1993–	Democratic	1946–	Albert A. Gore, Jr.

Facts About the Presidency

THE WHITE HOUSE

* John Adams was the first President to live in the White House. Since that time, this massive estate in Washington, D.C., has attracted the attention of people all over the world.

* Many rooms in the White House have a different names and unique purposes. Some of the many rooms are the Blue Room, the Red Room, and the Green Room.

* The President's office is called The Oval Office. And, this room is really shaped like an oval!

* Some people say that Lincoln's ghost haunts the old Lincoln bedroom in the White House. Although this room is not used on a regular basis, visiting dignitaries may get to spend the night in it.

OUTRAGEOUS ACTIONS

* Abraham Lincoln's son, Tad, kept a pet goat. When the goat began eating flowers in the White House garden, the Lincolns brought the unruly pet inside, where it slept on little Tad's bed!

* Theodore Roosevelt's children also had their share of unusual pets, including snakes, a macaw and a pony.

PRESIDENTIAL PRIVILEGES

* Whenever the President flies, he uses a personal plane, called Air Force One. The President and the Vice-President are not allowed to travel together, so the Vice-President does not get to use this plane very much.

* In addition to its 132 rooms, the White House has its own private bowling alley and movie theater!

* When the President and his family need a vacation, they can relax in the beautiful mountains of Maryland in the government-owned Camp David.

Glossary

Administration *noun* The President of the United States, the Vice-President, the Cabinet officers, and the departments they are in charge of.

Cabinet *noun* A group of people chosen by the leader of a government to serve as advisers and to be in charge of important departments of state.

campaign *noun* A series of actions for achieving a certain goal.

caucus *noun* A closed meeting of political party members to make policy decisions and choose candidates for office.

checks and balances *noun* A system of keeping the balance of power between different branches of a government.

citizen *noun* Someone who is a member of a country, either by birth or by choice.

Congress *noun* The United States Senate and House of Representatives.

constitution *noun* A set of laws or a plan under which a government or social group is organized.

convention *noun* A formal meeting of a group of people for a certain purpose.

delegate *noun* A person chosen to speak and act for another person or for a group: *He was chosen as the party's delegate to the conference.*

Democracy *noun* A form of government in which the people have the power, which they exercise directly or through representatives they have elected.

Democrat *noun* Someone who is a member of the Democratic Party.

elector *noun* A qualified voter.

Electoral College *noun* A group of electors chosen to elect the U.S. President and Vice-President.

executive *noun* The branch of government that manages affairs of a country and sees that its laws are put into effect.

Great Depression *noun* A period of extreme economic hardship during the 1930s.

inauguration *noun* The formal ceremony of placing someone in office.

incumbent *noun* Someone currently in office.

judicial *adjective* Of or ordered by judges.

legislative *adjective* Having power to make or pass laws.

majority *noun* More than half of the total: *A majority of the population voted for the bill.*

New Deal *noun* President Franklin D. Roosevelt's policies and programs for economic recovery and reform in the 1930s.

office *noun* A position of trust or responsibility.

paraphernalia *plural noun* The objects used in a given activity.

party (political) *noun* A group organized for political activity: *the Democratic Party.*

platform *noun* A statement of beliefs.

plank *noun* One of the articles of a political platform.

plurality *noun* The number of votes cast for the winner of an election when there is no majority: *He won by a plurality of the votes.*

politician *noun* Someone who runs for or holds an office in government.

primary election *noun* An early election to choose a political party's candidate for the regular election.

republic *noun* A form of government in which the voters elect their representatives and in which the leader is usually a president.

Republican *noun* Someone who is a member of the Republican Party.

slogans *noun* Phrases that express the goal or spirit of an organization or group.

statesman *noun* Someone who is skilled in government.

suffrage *noun* Right or privilege of voting.